DAILY INSPIRATION FOR EDUCATORS

POSITIVE THOUGHTS FOR EVERY DAY OF THE YEAR

VOLUME II

Jimmy Casas

ConnectEDD Publishing
Chicago, Illinois

Copyright © 2021 by Jimmy Casas.

This publication is available at discount pricing when purchased in quantity for educational purposes, promotions, or fundraisers. For inquiries and details, contact the publisher at info@connecteddpublishing.com

Published by ConnectEDD Publishing LLC
Chicago, IL
www.connecteddpublishing.com

Cover Design: Kheila Dunkerly

Daily Inspiration for Educators: Positive Thoughts for Every Day of the Year
Volume II/ Jimmy Casas. —1st ed.
Paperback ISBN 978-1-7361996-5-7

Introduction

Ever since I was a young boy, I have been a collector of quotations or clever sayings that made me think, or inspired me, or simply sounded interesting. In my very early years, I was a horrible student, so many of the quotes I picked up came from my sports heroes. I would read the sports section of the newspaper and check out biographies written about famous athletes and take note of anything they said that struck me as profound in any way. When I entered high school, I did no better academically; in fact, if anything, my performance went even further downhill. Yet, I remained always on the lookout for a well-stated quotation. I still remember one of my teachers had the following quote posted on her classroom wall: *"It's not my aptitude, but my attitude, that determines my altitude."* In addition, one of my coaches had this now-familiar saying posted in our locker-room: *"Whether you think you can, or think you can't, you're right."* Although most of my teachers regularly criticized my attitude toward them, their class, or school overall, inside of me was a voice that kept telling me I *did* have a good attitude and that it was my attitude (rather than my somewhat dubious intellect) that was going to one day propel me to succeed.

When I finally began experiencing at least some academic success while in college, I continued to be on the lookout for motivational quotations. At this point in my life, I took more of an interest in quotations from famous writers, thinkers, and historical leaders. I also began to realize that profound statements need not emanate solely from the mouths of "famous" people. One professor who I admired greatly often said things I thought were either wise or witty—or both. She also encouraged her students to think profound thoughts and whenever one of us said something she thought was particularly insightful, she would write it on the board in the front of the classroom and put it in quotation marks with the name of the person who said it underneath. I spent the entire semester trying to say clever things in the hopes that one day she would include something I said as the "student quote of the day." Unfortunately, nothing I uttered that semester merited formal recognition on her board, but I still remember the impact she made on me by emphasizing the importance of daily thoughts.

Although writing and speaking in public did not always come naturally to me, I kept at it and eventually I was able to author and co-author several books and I have now spoken in front of audiences throughout the country. After writing and speaking about all aspects of education for several years, one day I decided to begin sharing what I called a "Thought of the Day" through my various social media outlets. Most often, these "thoughts" were simply things I had been saying in my presentations or snippets from books I had written. I certainly never considered them very profound or even original, yet I was gratified by the response these daily thoughts received from those who followed them, and I realized that many people were just like me in that they were always on the lookout for a short saying that might make them think or might help carry them through their busy day. As a result of the positive feedback I was receiving from many educators, I have continued to send out daily thoughts about teaching, learning, leadership, or life in general for over four years. It has become a fun habit of mine to start my day and see the responses each daily thought elicits from other educators. Eventually, a close friend suggested I compile these thoughts into a small book of some sort and in 2021, I published Volume I of *Daily Inspiration for Educators: Positive Thoughts for Every Day*

JANUARY

JANUARY

We may not be able to let go of the fact that there will always be more to do, but we can let go of the guilt that can result from not getting it all done today. Let's not allow this year to be defined by the number of boxes we check off daily.

1

Never stop believing that something wonderful is about to happen.

2

JANUARY

Without reflection there is no growth. The power to grow lies in our ability and desire to reflect, and then be willing to commit to that change in order to become a better version of ourselves.

3

There will be days when teaching feels like a burden and we just aren't at our best. There will be days that learning feels the same way for some of our students. We just need to remember that.

4

JANUARY

As educators, our work is never finished. How we manage our time and energy will determine our effectiveness and overall impact. When we don't take care of ourselves, we run the risk of draining, rather than energizing, the very people we aim to serve.

5

Accept the fact that our lives will be filled with, "Oops" moments and, "What was I thinking?" moments. Let's model for our kids that failures don't have to equate to long-term doom. Commit to working through them with your head held high.

6

JANUARY

Successful educators are humbled by where they are from, never satisfied with where they currently are, and always inspired by where they aim to go. They are continuously taking another step toward their goals.

7

Students are inherently the most important people in our schools. If you're looking to redesign your school, courses, classrooms, etc., make sure to include students and give them more than just a seat at the table. Give them a voice at the table.

8

JANUARY

On occasion we must take time to declutter in order to get rid of the junk. Not from our closet or garage, but from our head. When we allow frustration, anger, and resentment to take up space in our head, we can't bring our best self to the day in front of us.

9

The foundation of healthy school cultures is found in the way adults interact with one another on a daily basis. How can we expect kids to be respectful and kind to one another if we, as adults, don't even treat each other in this manner?

10

JANUARY

It only takes one person to relate to your story. Honor your impact by tapping into your voice and past experiences. Everyone, including you, has something positive to contribute.

11

Sometimes we just need to get out of our own way. Appreciate the things you do well, acknowledge the things that you don't, and start believing that you can do better. Don't allow negativity and self-doubt to drain you and sabotage your success.

12

JANUARY

No student is unreachable. Every student is teachable. No student wants to fail. It's up to us to do whatever it takes to ensure they prevail. Be a champion for all kids.

13

Sometimes it takes the power of only two words for our students to begin to turn a dream into reality: "What if?" and "Why not?"

14

JANUARY

My experience has led me to believe that the way we discipline students in schools is directly related to the culture and climate of a school. Discipline that is fair, patient, compassionate, and loving leads to trust in adults and pride in the school.

15

When it comes to optimal team performance and cohesive relationships, vulnerability precedes trust, not the other way around.

—Dan Butler in *Permission to be Great: Increasing Engagement in Your School*

16

JANUARY

Effective educators are not afraid to make decisions. Talk with your colleagues, inform them of the process, ask questions, gather information, review the data, discuss it with your team, get a consensus, make a decision—and then act. Don't let the process become the product.

17

Don't try to convince others to "buy-in." It's not about selling something. Approach it in a way that makes others want to *invest* in what you are doing. That fosters commitment and is more sustainable—and healthier for the culture.

18

JANUARY

Most of what is complicated in our lives can be attributed to our own lack of self-awareness. Thus, we are creating most of our own issues. Begin today to give those close to you permission to help you identify your shortcomings.

19

Not once did a student ever walk into my office to complain that their teacher believed in them too much. But many did complain that they felt their teacher didn't like them. Be the teacher who keeps believing!

20

JANUARY

One of the biggest lessons I learned as a teacher and school leader was to never ask a student what his or her mom and dad would think or say if I called them. The sad truth was that too many students had lost a parent(s) or they were no longer in their life.

21

Don't kid yourself. Who you spend most of your time with matters. In fact, it matters a lot. Surround yourself with those who challenge you and remind you through their actions what love, joy, patience, compassion, and forgiveness looks like.

22

JANUARY

Here is the irony of it all. If we were asked from whom we have learned the most about being an educator, I think students could make the case it is from them. Observing, listening, talking, and working with students is their greatest gift to us.

23

For every minute you are angry you lose sixty seconds of happiness.
—Ralph Waldo Emerson

24

JANUARY

What if anytime a student or staff member was absent from school for a minimum of two days in a row teachers and administration would call to check on status, needs, and additional support? Kind, caring, and supportive gestures go a long way. It's the little things.

25

I often hear staff members talk about how they are like a family. Yet, they don't always know the names of every colleague. Do you know the name of every teacher, paraeducator, secretary, custodian, counselor, kitchen staff, etc. in your school? Never too late to start.

26

JANUARY

Trust is the most critical component in healthy cultures. At times, we need a safe place to vent in confidence. When that confidence is violated because we choose to share with someone else, it becomes gossip, which leads to an unhealthy culture.

27

One challenge I often see and experienced myself was asking staff and students their thoughts on a topic and receiving no response and then answering the question myself. Next time pair up, clarify the question, and then give more wait time to process, talk, and then list the responses.

28

JANUARY

We are not perfect beings. We will continue to make mistakes throughout our lifetime. When it happens, no amount of guilt will change the past. Instead, do your best to make it right and not repeat the error.

29

Regardless of our role in education, our students need us to bring our best selves to school every day. Just don't forget that our families need us to also bring our best selves home each night.

30

JANUARY

A team is not a group of people who work together. A team is a group of people who trust each other.
—Simon Sinek

31

FEBRUARY

FEBRUARY

Remember that every stage, field, court, pool, and mat is an extension of the classroom. The way we respond to and talk to students should mirror the same caring and respectful tone with the goal of creating a positive and successful experience for all kids.

1

It's not always enough to work hard on your own at something to be great. Sometimes you must allow others to help you in order to maximize your potential and impact. Who will you allow to help you today?

2

FEBRUARY

No matter how many times we tell students we care about them, it will never be enough unless we show them. To our students, our actions speak louder than our words.

3

It's been proven that multitasking is simply not effective or efficient. Juggling tasks back and forth ultimately takes longer and often is not done as effectively. Then why do we keep trying? Maybe it's time to refocus our attention on one task/person at a time.

4

FEBRUARY

Managing difficult people requires us to manage ourselves first.

5

If we're going to talk about achievement and opportunity gaps that are impacting students, then we need to include the instructional gap as well. Not to point fingers, but to recognize that we, as educators, also play a role in creating that gap.

6

FEBRUARY

A positive school culture begins by each one of us infusing a sense of pride into everything we do. It begins with us.

7

The most effective educators working in schools today all have this one thing in common: they believe in all kids all the time.

8

FEBRUARY

The best teachers are artists who know the science of teaching.
—Richard Bankert

9

Approach each situation with an understanding that at the heart of every problem is a conversation to be had. Invest time in others.

10

FEBRUARY

As educators continue to make decisions during these unprecedented times, remember that you don't have to be perfect to be effective. Gather input and lead with humility, transparency, and be flexible in your decision making. Nobody knows what tomorrow will bring.

11

Let's stop using the word "They" when referring to other members of our school community, especially when things are not going well or we're facing significant challenges. "We" are all in this together and our end result will be what we want it to be.

12

FEBRUARY

Make excellence your attitude. Make hard work your passion. Make serving others an experience...And watch how your life starts changing.

13

Are we intentional in doing our best to encourage others and give them hope? Let's do our best today to be vigilant in our words and deeds to help others feel valued and appreciated...and loved.

14

FEBRUARY

For most kids in this country, public education isn't their best shot. It is their only shot. We must get it right.
—Sir Ken Robinson

15

Don't let anyone ever take away your excellence. On those days when you don't feel your best, just remember: your personal excellence starts over every day.

16

FEBRUARY

Stay connected. The job of an educator can be all consuming. By reconnecting with mentors, former co-workers, and current colleagues, you will gain a greater appreciation for the work that you're doing and recognize how much you have grown over time.

17

Every student is one caring adult away from believing they can achieve greatness. You have the power to be that one caring adult today.

18

FEBRUARY

No one wins when we use demoralizing language that pits educators against parents or vice versa. It's not about us versus them, but rather us united as one.

19

I've never liked the tag "Hard-to-reach parents." Rather, I think those of us working in schools should reflect on our own practices so that we are not the "Hard to reach" ones. How are we intentionally building a sense of partnership with families so they want to connect with us?

20

FEBRUARY

The most effective educators not only expect the best from all kids, but they also see the best within all kids.

21

Do your words and actions inspire others?
Do you dismiss the needs of others?
Do your actions result in wellness or weariness?
Do you acknowledge the gifts of others?

22

FEBRUARY

Do the beliefs, attitudes, and interactions of staff with students and with each other scream: "I care about you! I know you can do this! You are important to me! I'm so glad to see you!"

23

The amount of support that some students need for even the smallest gains in learning can feel overwhelming at times. Hence, it's imperative that we cultivate a trusting, supportive culture so staff members never hesitate to ask for help.

24

FEBRUARY

The way we manage ourselves every day is what allows others to see our leadership skills in whatever position we hold. A title doesn't make anyone a leader. Inspiring others to want to lead does.

25

Always remember that if you are in the right place with the right people, you will always feel inspired. If you are not inspired, don't lose hope. It just means you are not in the right place...for now.

26

FEBRUARY

Some days all we can do for a student, colleague, or friend who is hurting is open our hearts and say, "I care about you, and I am here for you."

27

Imagine the impact that you make on learners when you answer a question with, "I don't know. Let's research this together."
—Marita Diffenbaugh in
L.E.A.R.N.E.R. - *Finding the True, Good, and Beautiful in Education*

28

MARCH

MARCH

We don't always have to change the entire world to leave a lasting legacy. Sometimes we can have the same impact by simply changing one person's world.

1

As necessary as it is to make learning experiences for students *challenging*, it is just as important that we make those experiences *enjoyable*.

2

MARCH

Parents, teachers, support staff, and administrators all have this one thing in common right now when it comes to their kids: trying to find that sweet spot between doing too little and doing too much. Kids are trying to figure it out, too.

3

No matter how many team building activities you do or how many facilitators you bring in to help you build a team, it will not give you the results you want unless you intentionally model what it means in getting to really know your colleagues.

4

MARCH

One of the biggest struggles many educators experience is the emotional toll that comes with meeting students where they are every single day. Not only do we give everything we have, but we also take everything away from it. Keep giving, but remember that you cannot do so unless you also take care of yourself.

5

It doesn't cost a single penny to reach out and greet someone with a friendly smile, lift a spirit with a sincere compliment, support others with a heartfelt note, or jolt those who are in a bad place with a blast of positive energy to get them through the day.

6

MARCH

If we want to create a culture of inclusivity, it's not enough to say that anyone is welcome, or we provide open access, or have full inclusion. For people to flourish and grow, we must also create a sense of belonging in which everyone feels welcomed and connected.

7

Expecting excellence from yourself is a choice. Striving for excellence each day is a lifestyle.

8

MARCH

Some days you must walk through the thick brush to get to the picnic. Don't let the prickles and thorns of the day deter you from finding and enjoying your picnic.

9

Every interaction is an opportunity to create an experience for others so that when they walk away, they "Carry the Banner" for you and your school. Those connections also inspire students and staff to want to come back...to class, to school, and work, each day!

10

MARCH

Even the biggest smiles sometimes hide the deepest pain. More than ever, educators need to watch over their students...and each other.

11

In a child's world, their issues are real regardless of what we, as adults, perceive to be the level of importance. Take time to listen.

12

MARCH

The more tasks we assign students and teachers to complete right now, the more check boxes we will create. Select and prioritize meaningful tasks and work or we will end up with an endless row of boxes filled with check marks and a culture of check...check...done.

13

Ultimately, people don't follow your words. They follow your integrity, your spirit. They don't follow what you say. They follow what you do and who you are.
—John Addison

14

MARCH

It's critical that we are intentional in making connections with kids so they never feel alone. It's just as critical that we also connect with one another. The work of an educator should never feel isolating.

15

The core of a school community is determined by the value that people bring to the organization. When we fail to acknowledge or dismiss the contributions of others, regardless how big or small, we miss an opportunity to strengthen our culture.

16

MARCH

When we ask for input and the responses are contrary to what we expected, perhaps we asked the right people who were willing to tell us what we needed to hear. A fresh perspective can lead to better decisions and often better results. Seek input.

17

Positive thoughts and feelings are not the result of positive outcomes in your life. They are the cause.

18

MARCH

Do your best today to leave the classroom with more energy than when you arrived.

19

Change isn't always scary. Sometimes not changing can be scary. It's a disservice to our teachers when we say they don't like change, or they fear change. What they fear is when we don't give them the support, resources, guidance, and *time* to change.

20

MARCH

One of the things that makes educators so special is that in many ways they are like another set of parents. They not only teach students lessons relating to reading, math, history, tech, languages, etc., but they also teach kids and young men and women how to live!

21

If we start our morning thinking it's not going to be a good day, we will likely be correct. Try to focus on one thing for which you are grateful, one thing that brings a smile to your face, or perhaps call or hug a loved one to start the day.

22

MARCH

Critic.
Talker.
Doer.
Inspirer.
At times we are all of these, but those who spend more time inspiring seem to be content and, in my experience, more enjoyable to be around.

23

We shouldn't always be satisfied when we meet expectations. At times we should expect to exceed expectations. To do so, we need to invest in and believe in our people. Only then can they begin to believe they can meet the challenges facing them.

24

MARCH

The pacing of a workday is directly related to workload distribution. So is stress and burnout. If students, teachers, support staff, principals, and superintendents are exhausted, it might be time to take something off our plates or provide more support.

25

When you take time to invest in areas of your life outside of work, you find more creativity, inspiration, and joy in serving others.
—William D. Parker in *Pause. Breathe. Flourish. - Living Your Best Life as an Educator*

26

MARCH

Don't put so much pressure on yourself today thinking you must do everything for everyone; rather, focus on doing one thing for someone. Your impact will be just as great... for them and for you.

27

People land where they land based on their past experiences. Sometimes those experiences carry deep wounds. When we take time to listen to their stories, we bring value to them as people and in turn they can begin to heal. Invest in those relationships.

28

MARCH

The next time you think about quitting, take a look around and see who is watching. What we model is what we get. The more we quit, the easier it becomes to quit. See it through to the end.

29

We can't ask students and staff to think outside the box and then turn around and tell them all the reasons why we can't make something work. Curiosity shouldn't have a lid—or a ceiling.

30

MARCH

You are the only one who can put limits on your own greatness. Commit today to live your life with no regrets.

31

APRIL

APRIL

When we focus on connections rather than behaviors, we give permission for our minds to recalibrate to the following: "Here is an opportunity to build a stronger relationship with a student and/or colleague."

1

Identify one student who is struggling and then commit to being a part of their success story this school year. At the end of the year when you look back, you will realize the impact it had on the student—and you!

2

APRIL

Live your 2% today! That's roughly thirty minutes of your entire day. You deserve that at the very minimum. Give it back to yourself free of guilt. Unplug from the stresses of life and find the joy in your day to inspire a healthier version of you.

3

If we find ourselves complaining about a task that needs to be completed or a meeting/training we are required to attend, then how can we get upset when a student displays the same attitude about an assignment or attending class?

4

APRIL

One way to make a positive, healthier impact as a teacher, principal, or school community is to identify where ineffective practices exist and then change them or remove them. This works in our personal lives as well.

5

Great teachers never **expect** anything but the absolute **best** from their students because they refuse to let them **become** anything less than the **best** they can possibly be.

6

APRIL

Every Student. Every Day. Whatever It Takes. is a critical mantra for any successful school. Just as important is to make sure we do whatever it takes for our teachers, support staff, and administration, too.

7

Inspiring educators are servant leaders; they think about the needs of others first and do whatever they can to illuminate their gifts rather than shine the light on themselves. How will you illuminate others today?

8

APRIL

Maybe we should pay closer attention to those we judge as mere dreamers. After all, their ideas and innovations are often the ones we dismiss as crazy, but the truth is, we all need a little craziness at times to believe we can succeed.

9

If we were to ask our students and staff what they personally need from us as teachers and administrators to feel valued, appreciated, confident, and excited to come to school every day to make a positive difference, what would they say? Let's take time to ask.

10

APRIL

If you want to build a ship, don't drum up people together to collect wood and don't assign them tasks and work, but rather, teach them to long for the endless immensity of the sea.
—Antoine de Saint-Exupery

11

The words that we say can never be taken back. So, choose wisely, especially during times of disagreement or conflict. Remember, it's more important to be kind than it is to be right.

12

APRIL

No matter how often and how much we punish kids at school it likely won't compare to the punishments some are experiencing at home. We can instead emphasize restorative practices that focus on relationship building and trust to influence behavior in positive ways.

13

Don't allow others to keep you from running your race. There will always be those who try to keep you standing on the sidelines, keeping you from being your best. Run your race today!

14

APRIL

As educators, we have the power to make a student walk out of class feeling better than they did before they walked in. The opposite is also true. Which will you choose today?

15

Use both quantitative and qualitative data to measure where you currently are and then work with your students, colleagues, and administration to determine where you want to be the next time. Just remember: progress over perfection.

16

APRIL

What if we changed In-School Suspension to In-School Support (Services)? Words matter. So does our mindset.

17

We all know the value and importance of self-care. However, caring for others is also a critical component of healthy cultures. Check on a student or colleague today and ask, "How are you doing? How can I help?"

18

APRIL

Let's focus on the "gots" rather than the "nots." When we get caught up focusing on what students and staff *don't* have rather than the skills and talents they *do* have, we create a self-fulfilling prophecy of helplessness.

19

Saying no to something that is not important is saying yes to something that is important.

20

APRIL

Positive and healthy change begins with self-change. Be the change today.

21

Cultures of compliance are not beneficial nor are they healthy over time. How can we help students and staff see the value, the good, and the benefit in something so they are more apt to invest in it rather than comply out of fear of being "punished"?

22

APRIL

Two simple things you can do today to connect with kids and colleagues: greet them by name when you see them and smile and say goodbye when they walk away. Sometimes it's the little things that say, "I care about you."

23

To influence the way children and young people think and behave in order to cultivate a healthy and positive school culture begins with us changing our own behavior. Model the way!

24

APRIL

If teachers and principals wrote a personal card or short letter to every one of their students or staff members this year, I wonder what the overall impact would be? One way to find out.

25

Building relationships with students and colleagues is a cornerstone of cultivating a healthy classroom and school culture. However, we can't forget the critical component of building a relationship with ourselves; and that involves caring for ourselves too.

26

APRIL

There are moments when you will have to ask students to do something and times when you will have to tell them what to do. The way they respond to you will depend on the sincerity of the relationship and level of trust you've built with them.

27

Leadership is not just about the ability to see what others aren't able to see. It's also about having the desire to do what others aren't willing to do.

28

APRIL

One benefit of creating a meaningful lesson plan is that it typically results in a positive learning experience for kids. When that happens, the additional benefit is that it creates a similar experience for educators as well. That is powerful teaching.

29

Championing for kids means envisioning who they can become, rather than dwelling over their shortcomings in the present moment.
—Emily Paschall in *Eyes on Culture: Multiply Excellence in Your School*

30

MAY

MAY

If we take the time to look a little closer and listen a little more, we may find out there are many stories yet to be told. Those stories not only allow others to feel valued and appreciated but can also inspire a sense of self-worth and belonging.

1

The pathway to a culture of excellence is never over. We are always on our way.

2

MAY

Great listeners are great observers. What do our observations tell us about how students and staff learn best?

3

Over the years I've come to believe that ineffective communication is the root cause of most cultural issues. What, when, where, and how we communicate is vital to our influence over others' morale, especially if we aim to inspire them to greatness.

4

MAY

Every meaningful relationship starts with a simple conversation, followed by another. And another. And another...

5

The greatest athletes in the world have coaches, yet educators are still trying to figure it out on their own. No matter how good we think we are at what we do, we can still get better, especially when we have someone to observe and coach us.

6

MAY

When our processes are not effective it usually means that our results will fall short of our expectations, causing a cultural undercurrent of negativity. It's also exhausting spending time trying to recover from cleaning up our own mistakes.

7

Stop whatever you're doing for a moment and ask yourself: Am I afraid of death because I won't be able to do this anymore?
—Marcus Aurelius

8

MAY

Don't strive to be better than everyone else today. Strive to be the best version of you.

9

Some students who disrupt class, who don't do their homework, who are late for class/ school are the same kids who want to eat lunch with you, talk to you during recess, or stop by after school to hang out. Some kids just need to feel connected before they are ready to learn.

10

MAY

It's not always the big stuff that is weighing us down, but the accumulation of a bunch of little things. Sometimes we must clean out the junk in our minds to start fresh, especially when we are frustrated with kids and colleagues.

11

When students struggle completing their work or accomplishing a task, we shouldn't look at it as if they can't do it, but simply that they need more practice. The same goes for us when we struggle.

12

MAY

If you forget your WHY, you'll forget your WAY. If you are working in schools and find yourself wondering if it's all worth it right now, please know it is. Rekindle your passion and purpose and look for the moments that warm your heart and ease your mind.

13

See every experience as part of a journey to who you are and who you will become. Life is not a constant. We are all works in progress.

14

MAY

Quality is never an accident; it is always the result of high intention, sincere effort, intelligent direction, and skillful execution.

—William Foster

15

Let your day be measured by the positive marks you leave on others today.

16

MAY

Effective educators do more than just share their vision with others. They are purposeful in striving to be a living example of what it takes to achieve it.

17

It's important to be transparent with information in order to **earn** the trust and confidence of others, but there are times it's more critical to maintain confidentiality in order to **keep** their trust and confidence.

18

MAY

Understand that teachers and administrators have a reason to be tired at the end of any school year, so when it comes to new programs or initiatives, recognize that it might be best to hold off for now and put your energy into improving what you are already doing.

19

Teachers understand the need to meet students where they are and take into account their different needs. Let's remember that teachers are no different. They, too, are at different levels and need supports delivered in a similar way to learn and grow.

20

MAY

Almost every school has an established set of beliefs and values statements that they have agreed to live by. However, what is missing are the agreed upon protocols for how to address staff who are not adhering to those statements.

21

Compassionate educators don't just use their words to lead, but behave in ways that draw others in and make them want to be around them.

22

MAY

When it comes to family engagement remember: when we speak to one family, we are really speaking to the entire community. We must treat all families as critical partners in our work with students.

23

A positive classroom environment is still the most critical element of ensuring that students feel safe, connected, and primed for academic success.

24

MAY

How we "show up" matters. It matters a lot. How we see ourselves in those moments also matters, even more so when we recognize we won't always "be ready" but are willing to give it our best shot regardless.

25

It's one thing to TELL others what we believe. It's another thing to SHOW them through our actions so they KNOW what we believe.

26

MAY

There are times when we stress over not being able to figure something out. Maybe the real reason we are stressed is because we've already figured it out and what we are actually worried about is how it will all turn out.

27

The next time you are rejected from achieving something that is important to you, shift your thinking. Maybe it's life's way of redirecting you to something better.

28

MAY

Life is full of treasures. Be sure to make time for what you treasure and remember to give time to those you treasure. Then watch how your life starts changing.

29

I can't imagine an educator ever looking back and saying to themselves, "I wish I would have given up on that student." I *can* imagine us looking back and wishing we hadn't. When we fight for kids, we always win, and I imagine we all could use a win today!

30

MAY

We are our best selves around people who encourage us to work hard and in environments in which we feel safe to take risks.

—Shane Saeed in *Be the Flame: Sparking Positive Classroom Communities*

31

JUNE

JUNE

Sometimes we must be willing to lean into a problem until we find a breakthrough. Our persistence will overcome resistance.

1

Imagine a school in which every student is welcomed with open arms and when they walk into the school or classroom a staff member is there to greet them and say, "It's so great to see you today!" Now ask yourself, "Is this your school?" *Every Student. Every Day.*

2

JUNE

Life-Fit: Rather than feel guilty about the things you think you should be doing, focus on the things that you can actually do and see if this fits you better.

3

Strive to create a culture of investment vs. a culture of compliance in order to bring value and meaning to the task at hand rather than have students and staff disengage from the task due to negativity or fear of failure.

4

JUNE

Children have never been very good at listening to their elders, but they have never failed to imitate them.
—James Baldwin

5

If you find yourself feeling like you are just standing in line, maybe it's time to choose a path where you can invest your heart, time, and energy in relationships that bring you the greatest joy.

6

JUNE

Every conversation or interaction we have with a student, or an event we attend, we get to choose how we see it: obligation or opportunity? Same can be said of our own families. Let's shift our thinking away from "have to" in favor of "get to."

7

One way to have less regrets in your life is to take advantage of the moments that come your way and never take them for granted.

8

JUNE

As educators we often define success for some students based on where they begin. For others it's how they finish. In reality, the start and finish is not nearly as important as the progress and growth they make in between. That is what should define their success...and ours, too.

9

Sometimes we allow our short-term emotions to negatively impact our thinking which, in turn, impacts our long-term decision making. When we limit our outlook, we limit our options.

10

JUNE

We can spend hours or even days trying to come up with a good idea, but if we then take that idea and implement it poorly, it can quickly become a bad idea. Process matters.

11

When it comes to clarity, leave nothing to chance. Not everything that is obvious in our minds is equally clear to others.

12

JUNE

When it comes to monitoring student progress and evaluation of staff, let's not focus solely on the grade or checking off boxes, but remember that our conversations with them play a critical part in helping us understand and evaluate their performance.

13

No matter how well we think we know our students and colleagues, we always seem to learn more about them during moments of personal challenges, despair, or crisis. A reminder to us all that we can always learn more about others by investing a little more time in others.

14

JUNE

Great teachers embrace learning rather than teaching as the fundamental purpose of the school.
—Rick DuFour

15

We often fail to put in the necessary time on the front end of a task, job, or conversation because "We don't have the time." Ironically, we then find the time to clean up a mess after the fact. We determine our **after** by clarifying our **before**.

16

JUNE

When it comes to change, things won't always turn out the way we hoped. But we can hit the reset button and shift our perspective, especially if we remember the best change comes from self-change.

17

Every time we make a decision that creates a negative undercurrent among students or staff, go back and examine these two areas: **Voice** and **Choice**. When we include others in the process, what we are saying is, "We value you."

18

JUNE

We should never stop believing in our youth even when they give us every reason to do so. Oftentimes they're just testing the adults who, from their experience, have quit on them in the past. Let's not let their behavior impact our attitudes about them.

19

One way to measure the depth of a healthy culture is by identifying the number of staff members who serve as "unofficial mentors" to their peers and students. When we invest our personal time in others, not only do we all bene-fit, so does our culture.

20

JUNE

Giving someone a seat at the table doesn't always equate to having a voice at the table. It may look good on paper, but does it serve the purpose you hoped it would?

21

Accepting feedback is the first step to having a voice, making change, and pursuing your dreams.

22

JUNE

Each day is a reminder that most of what the day brings is still up to us. There will always be exceptions, but regardless, we get to choose what we want our days to look like. Make it a great day today!

23

Sometimes the best teaching tool we have with students who struggle is a fresh start.

24

JUNE

Every kind act we do may not change the world, but it may change someone's world. Keep sharing kindness.

25

The path to greatness can sometimes appear lonely. If you look closer, you will see that others are cheering you on. Make sure you spend more time with those who lift you up rather than those who drag you down.

26

JUNE

Going through rough patches can allow us to understand our students when they go through those same patches. We are better off when we appreciate these moments rather than resent them.

27

When we stop allowing others to place limits on us, we begin to believe that **anything** is possible. When we stop placing limits on others, we help them believe that **everything** is possible.

28

JUNE

To **inspire** all students and staff to believe that anything is possible, then we must **aspire** to cultivate an environment in which they feel connected, confident, and capable.

29

Schools need to work for our students, not the other way around.
—Eric Sheninger in *Disruptive Thinking in Our Classrooms: Preparing Learners for Their Future*

30

JULY

JULY

No one is immune from fear. We all live with fear...fear of something. Fear is the one constant that can keep us from attaining what we may think is unattainable. Do your best to overcome your fears and regain control of what life has to offer.

1

Just Ask. Two simple words to remember to use the next time you see someone doing something that you don't understand, and it tempts you to pass judgement or make a false assumption.

2

JULY

When we invest time to get to know a student's personal story, we are more apt to not take their harsh behaviors personally. Same holds true for our friends and colleagues as well. We are all struggling in some capacity.

3

The only thing better than starting your day with a good compliment is by giving someone else a positive compliment to start their day.

4

JULY

Reflection is necessary for personal growth. When we are willing to revisit our decisions, look at our behavior, and see where we can be better, then we are well on our way to becoming the person we want to be.

5

We don't score any extra points by trying to resolve every problem on our own. Effective educators recognize the key to success is to share the work with others and take pride in the fact that together we can accomplish so much more.

6

JULY

Humility is not thinking less of yourself, but thinking of yourself less.
—C. S. Lewis

7

I worry sometimes about school counselors being "dumped on." This perception about them not teaching so they
have time to take on additional respon-
sibilities is a morale drainer. Counselors
are teachers. Let's allow them the time
and structure to do so.

8

JULY

Healthy school cultures share this in common: They don't define supervision as all eyes on students looking for any wrongdoings; instead, they actively engage and interact with all students in a genuine manner to foster positive relationships.

9

Not every situation is an emergency, but we can fall into the trap of treating them as such. Slowing down helps us prioritize and allows us to regulate the level of urgency it requires of us. This can bring a sense of steadiness to every situation.

10

JULY

Make sure to always spend time with people who look forward to spending time with you.

11

Once you realize what truly matters, you begin to understand how many things truly do not. Focus on what matters most.

12

JULY

The key to approaching difficult conversations is to begin by asking questions. It is always best to try and better understand a situation before expressing our thoughts and concerns.

13

Not all information that a student shares with us in confidence is meant to be shared with our colleagues. It's important to filter what to share and who needs to know in order to protect confidentiality and maintain trust.

14

JULY

It's not what is poured into a student that counts, but what is planted.
—Linda Conway

15

Life's most persistent and urgent question is, 'What are you doing for others?
—Martin Luther King, Jr.

16

JULY

Sometimes we need to tell students where to look. The key is to not tell them what to see.

17

There is always light, if only we're brave enough to see it. If only we're brave enough to be it.
—Amanda Gorman

18

JULY

Asked a principal yesterday how she wanted to be remembered when she retired and she responded, "One who loved her students and staff into learning—it always starts with loving them and the rest will come." Something tells me she made a difference.

19

The best teachers don't always teach the lesson plan. They see the moments when they need to stop and step aside and teach manners, respect, kindness, patience, forgiveness, or how to show appreciation for others. Simply put, they teach life and model how to live it.

20

JULY

You should feel good when students go home and talk about the lesson you taught. You will feel even better if they talk about how you challenged them to think, about the conversations that took place, and how you made them feel.

21

Maybe things aren't happening **to** us, but rather **for** us. Life has a funny way of keeping us grounded and reminding us of the important things in our lives. Keep a fresh perspective.

22

JULY

One way we can manage student discipline more effectively is to make sure students feel their voice is the most important one in the conversation.

23

People's outward expressions don't always align with their internal feelings. Sometimes we just need to be mindful that others may be dealing with internal struggles that they are not sure how to manage.

24

JULY

When we try something new and it works, it feels great and often gives us the confidence to try something new again. When we fail it can be painful and make us doubt ourselves. Remember, tough times are about making us different—in a better way.

25

Don't spend time worrying about being wrong. Spend your energy trying to figure out what you learned from being wrong.

26

JULY

We cannot change what we are not aware of, and once we are aware, we cannot help but change.
—Sheryl Sandberg

27

One positive practice for managing student behavior is for adults to recognize we won't always get it right when handling situations. When we don't, we need to apologize, try to make it right, and ask for forgiveness.

28

JULY

It's extremely difficult for students to learn when they believe the adults at school don't like them. The key is to show compassion, try and understand why they feel that way, and then work with them in a way that changes their perception of us.

29

We must do our best not to be deterred by failure or the unknown, but rather remain motivated by hope and faith. By doing so, we can inspire others to do the same. If we don't believe we can make a difference in this world, rest assured we won't.

30

JULY

Every student. Every day. Whatever it takes. Let's make sure to replicate this mindset for our teachers, administrators, and support staff as well. We are all better when we have each other's back.

31

AUGUST

AUGUST

The most effective educators believe this one thing: *Everyone Matters.*

1

To lead graciously, sometimes we must be willing to admit to ourselves that we don't know what to do...and then be willing to ask others for help.

2

AUGUST

A teacher shared a great reminder with me that all kids need two things: to be praised and to be polished. Some just need more of our time, attention, and love. Bring the polish every day.

3

Show me a school that pits teachers against administrators or vice versa and the result will be an unhealthy culture. A healthy culture is inspired when administrators and other staff members advocate for and support one another in their collective quest to make a positive impact on students.

4

AUGUST

How many times a day do we ask students and staff how they're doing and the response we get is "Great!" Now ask yourself how many times you just walk on by? Do we really care? Next time, stop and ask what made it great. Let's invest our time and show we care.

5

On the days we find ourselves doubting our purpose, we must look closely for the small moments that bring us joy. They are all around us—although some days we may have to squint.

6

AUGUST

Every kid deserves a champion. What if we were to ask students to identify a staff member who has championed for them? Then ask them to write or create a video explaining how and then deliver the message to staff members. Adults need champions, too.

7

When a family reaches out to their child's school in their time of need that signals that the culture of the school is what that family needs at that time. That is a beautiful thing. Every school should strive to be that place of connection.

8

AUGUST

What if we shifted the conversation from "rules" to "agreements"? Giving students a voice and ownership in establishing classroom expectations promotes positive accountability and allows them to own the principles they agreed to.

9

Why is it when a teacher goes from the classroom into administration, they are in danger of becoming a "they?" Let's commit to staying united and reminding ourselves that we are still a "we" and always will be.

10

AUGUST

When we personally reach out and invest in our students and colleagues, we send a sincere message to them that says, "I see you. I value you. I am here for you." They know it. They feel it. They need it. Reach out to someone today.

11

The most effective educators not only teach meaningful content, but they also model how to treat missteps as opportunities for teaching and learning based on dignity and respect.

12

AUGUST

Every day is a day we won't get back. Rather than look backwards and lament about missed opportunities, do your best to look ahead and strive to be tomorrow...today.

13

When students misbehave, it is more than just an interruption to the teaching taking place. It is also a form of communication. Getting to the root cause of misbehavior is essential if we want to support students in correcting it.

14

AUGUST

Student outward expressions don't always align with their internal feelings.
—Jimmy Casas and Joy Kelly in *Handle with Care: Managing Difficult Situations in Schools with Dignity and Respect*

15

The next time your own child tells you something that frustrates you, worries you, hurts you, or angers you, remember: be grateful they are at least talking to you. How you respond might determine who or if they talk to anyone the next time.

16

AUGUST

As educators, we must recognize that we won't always get it right. There will be times when students and parents remind us that even when we get it wrong, our humility can guide us to make things right again.

17

A sense of pride doesn't have to be dependent on achieving your goals. Setting a goal and working towards it can be just as rewarding, especially when it is accompanied by hardships overcome along the way.

18

AUGUST

Leadership can be about sitting back and allowing others to talk. It's also about knowing when to step forward and have the courage to say what others are not willing to say, but doing it in a caring and respectful way.

19

One characteristic of successful people is that their mindset begins with not only a **can do** attitude, but a **will do** attitude. What will you do today?

20

AUGUST

The most effective educators know that difficult conversations are not something they can outsource to someone else.

21

As a teacher, administrator, or parent, what are two things you expect your students, staff, or children to do on a daily basis? Now ask yourself, "Am I modeling the same expectations and/or behaviors?" What we model is what we get.

22

AUGUST

Every contribution, regardless of how big or small, is an opportunity to value what people bring to an organization. When we dismiss or fail to acknowledge students', staff, or volunteers' efforts, we miss an opportunity to strengthen our culture.

23

Do your best to live the life of excellence you imagined. Not perfection... but your very best.

24

AUGUST

When we don't get the results that we wanted, rather than blame others, we should always look internally first and ask ourselves how we may have contributed to the problem.

25

When teachers and school leaders teach and lead from their heart and soul, with compassion and integrity, we not only influence kids and adults to be better students and teachers, but also inspire them to be better people as well.

26

AUGUST

Sustainable change takes root in the foundation of a changed heart. We all need to change at times in order to become better versions of ourselves.

27

If you scan the world around you for negativity, you will certainly find it. Just don't let it hijack your positivity.

28

AUGUST

As schools begin to lay out plans for the fall, be mindful of where and with whom you share your frustrations. Kids don't need to hear adults complaining about the decisions being made and when kids complain, let's model what it means to be the voice of reason.

29

As a teacher, you are remembered forever; how you are remembered is up to you.
—Vickie Gill

30

AUGUST

We can't meet higher standards of learning if classroom management is our primary focus. Successful instruction, which addresses students' developmental and intellectual needs, is the highest form of classroom management. When students are actively engaged, they rarely create havoc.
—Rick Wormeli

31

SEPTEMBER

SEPTEMBER

Effort matters...
Words influence...
Interactions impact...
Actions inspire...
Bring your best today!

1

Asking for help is not a weakness. It's actually a sign of confidence, humility, and self-awareness. Reach out and ask someone today, "Could you help me with this?"

2

SEPTEMBER

Almost every dilemma you encounter as a classroom teacher or a school or district leader will have a solution; it just doesn't have to be you who comes up with it. Trying to fix it all alone will just leave you feeling depleted and exhausted.

3

Whether we recognize it or not, our every word and deed have the potential to either add positively to the school culture or not. It's that simple. What will you add today to contribute to a positive school culture?

4

SEPTEMBER

When students are disrespectful, the greater respect we need to extend in return. When we respond disrespectfully, louder, or more harshly, we are not teaching them, and we definitely will not reach them.

5

Healthy classrooms and healthy meetings help nurture an environment that values curiosity. Do your best to provide opportunities for students and staff to ask questions and share their thoughts.

6

SEPTEMBER

Get used to the fact that not everything always goes as planned. Life is unpredictable. People will disappoint us. How we conduct ourselves in these moments will either inspire or deflate others. Let's allow them to recover from their mistakes.

7

We all have our good days, bad days, proud moments, and not-so-proud moments. What we can do is commit to being just a little better each day. A better friend, a better colleague, a better spouse, and yes, a better educator.

8

SEPTEMBER

One way we often get in our own way is when we make decisions and take action based on feelings rather than facts.

9

When we operate from absolutes, the opportunity to strengthen our relationships with students is often overlooked.

10

SEPTEMBER

Sadly, there are still too many examples of adults punishing kids in school. As educators, we need to use discipline as a means to teach, provide guidance, and influence students in a positive way.

11

We cannot say we value student voice and then try to shut it down when their message is uncomfortable or potentially controversial.

12

SEPTEMBER

We need caring administrators and teachers now more than ever to work together to do the right things the right way for all kids...and for each other.

13

It isn't enough to tell people they need to get better. We need to show them what better looks like and then provide them the necessary ongoing coaching, resources, and guidance to help them be better.

14

SEPTEMBER

Teacher Growth is closely related to pupil growth. Probably nothing within a school has more impact on students in terms of skills development, self-confidence, or classroom behavior than the personal and professional growth of their teachers.

—Roland Barth

15

If you want to gain the trust of others, then do what you say you are going to do. Be where you say you will be. Say what you mean; mean what you say. Be dependable. Be reliable. Be great.

16

SEPTEMBER

We shouldn't get our feelings hurt if we ask for input and the responses are contrary to what we expected. Recognize this as a sign that perhaps we asked the right people who were willing to tell us just what we needed to hear.

17

One issue impacting school culture is the negative behavior of some staff members. To improve morale for all staff, we need to understand why people behave negatively and more importantly, work to address those issues rather than ignore them.

18

SEPTEMBER

In those moments when you can't find the right words to say, simply speak from the heart. Others will appreciate your genuineness and sincerity in your voice and your approach.

19

Sometimes we fall into the trap of feeling like we must resolve an issue as soon as it's brought to our attention. It's OK to ask for time to process the information and then revisit the conversation at a later time. This often brings clarity to the problem.

20

SEPTEMBER

It's important that we continue to take inventory of our own learning and do our best to learn new things, so we never forget what it feels like to struggle at something new. The experience will remind us how some kids feel at school some days.

21

Screw ups are a part of life. Just remember to always be hard on the mistakes in order to correct them, but soft on the person in order to build them up.

22

SEPTEMBER

A sincere apology can go a long way in building a trusting relationship, especially if the result is a change in our actions for the better.

23

Staff members could benefit from having a "calming room" to get away from the daily stresses they encounter. Providing a space for staff to take even just a few minutes to experience some peace will reap benefits.

24

SEPTEMBER

Focus on students' strengths rather than wrongdoings. Their mistakes should not negatively define who they are or their value within the school community.

25

Be a gatekeeper for students and staff. Have the ability and integrity to keep private, personal information confidential. Understand what is your news to share with others and what is not.

26

SEPTEMBER

Sometimes we just need to stop talking and be quiet. Sit in silence and try to get comfortable with the quiet between you and others. See your silence as a form of communication that gives others time to process and respond.

27

Behind every successful student is an adult who championed that student.

28

SEPTEMBER

When we model a strong, balanced work ethic it serves as a reminder to our kids that if they make hard work their passion, then they will be successful no matter what career path they choose.

29

Beliefs are not enough; if we are interested in improvement, our behaviors must align with our beliefs.
—Dan Butler in *Permission to be Great: Increasing Engagement in Your School*

30

OCTOBER

OCTOBER

When we work across boundaries, we actually leverage each other's talents and, therefore, we are more productive. We are always better together than alone if we want to be.

1

The healthiest cultures not only have shared commitments, but behave in ways that reflect those commitments.

2

OCTOBER

We should all strive to know the names of all our students and pronounce them correctly. Close enough doesn't cut it. Pronouncing names correctly is a sign of respect.

3

Being accessible doesn't ensure that our availability is fruitful. The spirit of our accessibility makes the difference and signals how accessible we want to be. Students should feel they are the reason for our work rather than an interruption of it.

4

OCTOBER

We can call kids out in front of class-mates. We can raise our voices at them and/or punish them to gain compliance. This approach does not change student behavior. It simply teaches them how we will weaponize our authority to maintain power.

5

When students lash out, it's their way of telling us that things are out of order for them. The louder a student gets, the quieter and softer adults need to be. The more disrespectful a student becomes, the greater respect we need to extend.

6

OCTOBER

Discipline that is fair, patient, compassionate, and loving leads to trust among students and adults and pride in the school. Discipline that is random, unpredictable, intolerant, and punitive results in anger, mistrust, and withdrawal. Which path will you choose?

7

Students are going to have missteps. They're going to make poor choices and use bad judgment. They're going to disrupt and interfere with the learning process even when that's not their intent. We can't assume that misbehavior reflects their true character.

8

OCTOBER

While extending patience to a student or a staff member who has violated a rule or policy is important, so too is granting patience to the process to ensure we respond fairly. Sometimes we need to slow down in order to get it right.

9

When students struggle to regulate their emotions and reactions, we need to raise our compassion, not our voices.

10

OCTOBER

Students do not have to be right and have the last word; neither do we. It's the most unproductive combination imaginable in any relationship. Know when to pull back and let a student have the last word—at least at that moment. Avoid the argument trap.

11

People can't fix what they don't see. Being honest and direct with others in a kind, caring, and thoughtful way can prevent a minor issue from ballooning into a major one. Take the necessary time today to initiate a conversation you've been avoiding.

12

OCTOBER

In our effort to dodge difficult conversations, our avoidance may actually condone and even accommodate bad behavior. Being a champion for others means interrupting that pattern of avoidance in order to help them become a better version of themselves.

13

Teaching is not about us being brilliant; it is about students being brilliant.
—Tom Newkirk

14

OCTOBER

Great leaders are great teachers at heart and great teachers are great leaders. Both help others discover for themselves what *they* want to do rather than what *we* want them to do.

15

People who feel valued and appreciated will always do more than what is expected. Who are some people you value and how can you show your appreciation today?

16

OCTOBER

While we all have experienced feeling slighted or disrespected by a student at one time or another, most often the student's behavior really has nothing to do with us. When we are offended easily, we rob ourselves of peace and joy.

17

We spend an enormous amount of time and energy helping children identify their missteps and learning from their mistakes. Do we afford the same to adults who have fallen short of expectations? For our people to get better, we must support them.

18

OCTOBER

We can talk about our mission, vision, and values and post them all over the building, but if we don't live them on a daily basis then they are merely words about words.

19

Poor leadership impacts everything and everyone. So does great leadership. How will you lead today?

20

OCTOBER

A school or district leader who loves their work can inspire others to aspire for a leadership position. Consider it one more way we can serve others.

21

We must ask ourselves, "Do I have enough information to make decisions? Am I making decisions too quickly without the necessary information or conducting the necessary interviews?" Leadership isn't easy—asking tough questions and holding people accountable isn't easy either. Still, we do it.

22

OCTOBER

Rarely will we make everyone happy. We need to make peace with the fact that other people will (falsely) talk about situations and we won't be able to respond. Being on the receiving end of such false accusations about the way a situation was handled is never fun. We must press on and continue to do the right thing regardless.

23

The goal within activities should be to level up participants in simple but meaningful ways; strengthening an athletic or fine arts skill, developing communication and leadership proficiencies, and cultivating intrinsic motivation to help them improve.

24

OCTOBER

Effective educators focus on the 3 P's:
1. They work with others as **Partners.**
2. They implement a **Process.**
3. They deliver a final **Product.**

25

Our students will need guidance more often than not, but that is very different from needing direction. Let's give them, within the safe and supportive school environment, the autonomy they need so they can learn to lead themselves.

26

OCTOBER

If we are not directly telling staff members what we expect in terms of how we are going to talk to students, we are leaving it to chance. And, chances are, students will be spoken to in negative ways that you may never know about.

27

As a family we must be willing to raise the level of awareness and accountability when one of our own is speaking negatively about a student or colleague. We must be willing to say, "I'm not very comfortable with the way you are speaking about..."

28

OCTOBER

Students need to understand why they are learning, and it is respectful to share this information with them.
—Marita Diffenbaugh in
L.E.A.R.N.E.R. - Finding the True, Good, and Beautiful in Education

29

We should never underestimate the importance of building character with our students. Who they become as people because of their time with us is equally as important to how they perform academically.

30

OCTOBER

As you close out another month, remember to honor your accomplishments. Honor your gifts. Honor those who have come before you. Honor the stories. Honor your impact.

31

NOVEMBER

NOVEMBER

We can raise expectations without raising our voices or the level of fear. The young brain will respond much better to teaching, directing, and encouraging than yelling, blaming, and ridiculing. The stage, court, or field are an extension of the classroom. Teach them.

1

It's critical we take time to listen to others when working through difficult or less-than-ideal situations. We bring harm to our culture when we ignore or reject the opinions, experiences, or ideas of others. Let's ensure that everyone has a voice.

2

NOVEMBER

When a student has broken down and is yelling, crying, and saying inappropriate things, focus on the emotion more than the words they are using. Too often we listen only to the words, looking to place blame, rather than responding to the hurt and the pain.

3

If people are always asking for permission, then maybe we haven't done a good enough job of building capacity. Rather than label others as "bothersome or annoying," let's reflect on what we can do to inspire them to have the confidence to act.

4

NOVEMBER

Can we own the fact that as adults we don't always get it right? How many times have we spoken with students about their behavior, yet failed to recognize that we sometimes need to work on our own self-management as well?

5

Are the people or the things that are most important to you getting your best self? If not, what are you waiting for?

6

NOVEMBER

When a child feels connected, confident, and capable, then anything is possible.

7

Model educators never ask people to do things they are unwilling to do themselves. They do not blame others and always take responsibility for their own actions. They are committed to serving others, rather than merely doing a job. Which educator will you be today?

8

NOVEMBER

Students are more likely to put forth their best effort when they have a legitimate voice in the process. The same holds true for teachers and support staff. Input matters.

9

Look around and you will notice that the best educators intentionally surround themselves with the best. They are comfortable with who they are and never feel threatened by others who are viewed as highly talented.

10

NOVEMBER

A great teacher changes everything. Ask any student who has had one. Teachers matter. Thank you for serving as a teacher.

11

Sometimes we just need to give others permission to help us be better. Ask students and staff to help you see what you don't see yourself so you can be the best version of you.

12

NOVEMBER

How we respond to the daily challenges we face is our choice. Do your best today to not allow your current circumstances to impact your mood, attitude, and/or interactions with others in a negative way. Behave your way to a better day.

13

You may work faster alone, but you always accomplish more meaningful outcomes when you include others on your journey.
—William D. Parker in *Pause. Breathe. Flourish. - Living Your Best Life as an Educator*

14

NOVEMBER

One thing all effective educators know about themselves is that they don't have all the answers…and they are not afraid to admit it to others.

15

In the best classrooms, every student feels like the favorite student. In the best schools, every teacher and support staff also feel like the favorite. Let's treat everyone like we treat our favorites.

16

NOVEMBER

One thing we must learn to accept as educators is that there will always be outliers—the ones who love you regardless of your mistakes and the ones who will never like you no matter your contributions. Regardless, we must continue to teach and lead with integrity.

17

Create a vision, share it, and then be a living example of what it takes to achieve it.

18

NOVEMBER

When we try to better understand the reason behind the behaviors of others, we are more equipped to provide guidance, influence thinking and emotions, and help frame situations in ways that help them discover a more positive path forward.

19

Being an educator today requires a great deal of fortitude, especially for those who aim to influence the status quo. If your resolve is currently being tested, it's because you refuse to settle. Keep believing in yourself.

20

NOVEMBER

Telling others how they can be better is very different from working with them to become better.
—Emily Paschall in *Eyes on Culture: Multiply Excellence in Your School*

21

In those moments when you find yourself questioning a decision you made, just remember, at least you had the courage to make a decision. We won't always get it right, but we also take a risk when we don't make a decision for fear of making the wrong decision.

22

NOVEMBER

As teachers, we have an opportunity to cultivate an environment in which every student is able to leave a positive mark on their school community. Principals can do the same for staff. By changing our perspective and our actions, we can impact a legacy.

23

Those who aspire for greatness are never deterred by the doubters. When told by others they won't succeed, they often respond with one simple phrase: "Watch me."

24

NOVEMBER

Work fills such a large part of our lives. If we want to be truly satisfied in our work, then our work must be meaningful. And the only way to achieve that is to love what we do and be passionate about what we do.

25

There will always be more work to do, more deadlines to meet, another situation to resolve, and an email inbox that rarely reaches zero. Stop feeling guilty because you can't get it all done. Let it go. It will still be there tomorrow, and it will all work out.

26

NOVEMBER

Receiving feedback is critical to changing our practice for the better and we cannot let our pride get in the way of giving students a voice in the classroom.
—Shane Saeed in *Be the Flame: Sparking Positive Classroom Communities*

27

At the heart of every problem is a conversation to be had. We cannot fall into the trap of deflecting conversations about concerns or issues that are brought to our attention. Be willing to have more dialogue to truly understand the issue(s) at hand.

28

NOVEMBER

I would rather assume the best about students and be proven wrong, than assume the worst about them and be proven right.
—Jeff Zoul

29

There are times when some adults in the classroom, on the field or stage, or leaders of the school use intimidation, fear, coercion, or ridicule to get others to conform to their expectations. Let's commit to being better than that today—and every day.

30

DECEMBER

DECEMBER

No matter how many times you dismiss a compliment, avoid a pat on the back, or give the credit to others, people who value hard work know who you are and will always appreciate you and the work you do. Own it with pride.

1

How we respond and reach out to those who are in need can make all the difference in the lives of those who, at that moment, need our very best. As an educator ask yourself, "At this moment, am I touching the hearts of others the best that I can?

2

DECEMBER

The best part about being an educator is that every day we have an opportunity to change the trajectory of the life of a child. Stay vigilant; today may be that day.

3

For educators, our legacy is not about personal success, but rather the significance and impact we have on others.

4

DECEMBER

As adults, when we make mistakes or bad decisions, we often want others to not judge us, forgive us, give us a second/third chance, and treat us in a kind and positive way moving forward. Kids want the same thing from us. Let us always extend grace—to ourselves as well as those with whom we interact.

5

Even the most challenging students need us to believe in them. **Believe** that they care. **Believe** that they can. **Believe** that they will.

6

DECEMBER

All kids have greatness hidden inside them. It is the job of an educator to help find and unleash that greatness.
—Eric Sheninger in *Disruptive Thinking in Our Classrooms: Preparing Learners for Their Future*

7

Oftentimes we only hear the voices around us when we should be paying more attention to the voice within us. Always remember that your voice matters, too.

8

DECEMBER

Teaching and coaching others is more than just giving directives. It is about instilling confidence, supporting learning, and helping bridge feelings of loss, inadequacy, or fear with opportunity, possibility, and relief.

9

It's not only what you know about your students and staff, but how you treat your students and staff that determines the health and productivity of your classroom and school culture.

10

DECEMBER

Remember, sometimes when students or staff come to us to share a personal struggle, they just want us to understand what they need at that moment without judgment.

11

All we can control today is what we do to be better and do better than we were and did yesterday. Live your excellence today!

12

DECEMBER

Regardless of what your role or title is at work, do your very best to bring your best each day. Then make sure you do the same when you go home. Your family deserves to see the best version of you.

13

As an educator, your principal job is to create environments in which *others* can do great things.

14

DECEMBER

It's easy to fall into the trap of labeling dissatisfied parents as difficult parents. What if we reframed the way we thought about them as simply parents in difficult situations who in that moment need our help?

15

The best days are often the ones we approach like we've decided to go for it.

16

DECEMBER

The phrase "What is best for students" is often used. However, as educators we come with different perspectives on what this means. Therefore, it is critical we have a process, so all staff can have a voice in defining what we mean by "What is best."

17

How many students are walking our hallways feeling invisible and in some cases, hopeless? Imagine the level of care they would receive if they had a "Handle with Care" sticker attached to them. Would their school experience be different?

18

DECEMBER

There will be days when people judge you, criticize you, and treat you in ways that are unfair. In those moments, stay the course; don't let them take away your excellence.

19

People often make decisions and take action based on feelings rather than facts.
—Jimmy Casas and Joy Kelly in *Handle with Care: Managing Difficult Situations in Schools with Dignity and Respect*

20

DECEMBER

Detentions can have tremendous benefits when used as a restorative practice. Rather than using them as a punishment, utilize them to connect, build a relationship, assess a student's understanding of content, re-teach, build confidence, and just talk.

21

We are all one experience away from losing our way and losing hope, but we are also one experience away from changing a life for the better and inspiring others to greatness.

22

DECEMBER

You are a leader:
1. When you have a disposition about you that others recognize and want to emulate.
2. When people notice your tendency to always see the best in others.
3. When you take great pride in and care deeply about your school.

23

Educators need breaks from teaching just as much as students need breaks from learning. Both need time to "play", socialize, move, re-energize, and reduce stress.

24

DECEMBER

Take people as they are: Accept that people will disappoint you. They won't work as hard as you think they should, they won't meet the timeline you establish, and they may not carry themselves in the manner you expect. Love, trust, and forgive them anyway.

25

It can be frustrating when students submit substandard work, accept their finished work as "good enough," complain to others that the request is unfair or give up altogether. It can be even more frustrating when we do the same as adults.

26

DECEMBER

If you want to test your memory, try to recall what you were worrying about one year ago today.
—E. Joseph Cossman

27

Sometimes I think we put so much emphasis on managing kids that we lose sight of what really matters. Rather than focus on a student's behavior, maybe we should focus on understanding the reason for the behavior.

28

DECEMBER

The next time we get frustrated at a student who is texting in class during a lesson, just look around at the adults in a professional learning session. The issue is not the phones. It's us.

29

Rise above the little things. There's a reason they are called little things.

30

DECEMBER

Students will remember how we treated them long after they forget what we taught them.

31

About the Author

Jimmy Casas served twenty-two years as a school leader. He is a best-selling author, speaker, leadership coach, and a state and national award-winning principal. Under Jimmy's leadership, Bettendorf High School was named one of the best high schools in the country three times by Newsweek and U.S. News and World Report.

Jimmy was named the 2012 Iowa Principal of the Year and was runner-up NASSP 2013 National Principal of the Year. In 2014,

Jimmy was invited to the White House to speak on the Future Ready Pledge. Finally, in 2015, he received the Bammy Award for the National Principal of the Year. Jimmy is the author of several books, including *What Connected Educators Do Differently, Start. Right. Now. – Teach and Lead for Excellence, Culturize: Every Student. Every Day. Whatever It Takes., Stop. Right. Now. 39 Stops to Making Schools Better*, and *Live Your Excellence: Bring Your Best Self to School Every Day*. He recently co-authored *Handle with Care: Managing Difficult Situations in Schools with Dignity and Care* with Joy Kelly.

Jimmy currently serves as an adjunct professor for Drake University, teaching courses in educational leadership. Finally, he is the owner and CEO of J Casas & Associates, an educational leadership company aimed at providing world-class professional learning services for educators across the country.

More from ConnectEDD Publishing

Since 2015, ConnectEDD has worked to transform education by empowering educators to become better-equipped to teach, learn, and lead. What started as a small company designed to provide professional learning events for educators has grown to include a variety of services to help teachers and administrators address essential challenges. ConnectEDD offers instructional and leadership coaching, professional development workshops focusing on a variety of educational topics, a roster of nationally recognized educator associates who possess hands-on knowledge and experience, educational conferences custom-designed to meet the specific needs of schools, districts, and state/national organizations, and ongoing, personalized support, both virtually and onsite. In 2020, ConnectEDD expanded to include publishing services designed to provide busy educators with books and resources consisting of practical information on a wide variety of teaching, learning, and leadership topics. Please visit us online at connecteddpublishing.com or contact us at: info@connecteddpublishing.com

Recent Publications:

Live Your Excellence: Action Guide by Jimmy Casas

Culturize: Action Guide by Jimmy Casas

Daily Inspiration for Educators: Positive Thoughts for Every Day of the Year by Jimmy Casas

Eyes on Culture: Multiply Excellence in Your School by Emily Paschall

Pause. Breathe. Flourish. Living Your Best Life as an Educator by William D. Parker

L.E.A.R.N.E.R. Finding the True, Good, and Beautiful in Education by Marita Diffenbaugh

Educator Reflection Tips Volume II: Refining Our Practice by Jami Fowler-White

Handle With Care: Managing Difficult Situations in Schools with Dignity and Respect by Jimmy Casas and Joy Kelly

Disruptive Thinking: Preparing Learners for Their Future by Eric Sheninger

Permission to be Great: Increasing Engagement in Your School by Dan Butler

Be the Flame: Sparking Positive Classroom Communities by Shane Saeed